dismantled

nirali amin

to those who nurtured me,
mom and dad

a torrid desert arose;

water, nowhere to be found

and yet, a flower grows

-    *women*

introduction

life is all about giving back to the greater good. being raised as a child of immigrant parents, this is one value that was instilled within me since childhood. life is not about making the most money and owning the best things. life is much greater than that.

my parents were married in india. however, my mother was a united states citizen at the time but my father did not receive a visa to come to the states until a year after they had been married. this means that my parents spent the first year of their marriage on two separate spectrums of the globe.

once my father was finally able to come to the states, both he and my mother decided that they wanted to start a future in texas, away from everyone else. they both drove to texas and had nothing but a small amount of money along with a car that had an old comforter set within it. for a while, they both lived in that car until they had saved enough money from working minimum wage jobs to afford a small apartment in dallas, texas. later, my mother decided that her working at walmart and my father working at ups was not going to cut it and that they deserve more for their future family. therefore, my mother obtained two more minimum wage jobs in order to put my father through engineering school. near the last year of my father's time in school, my mother became pregnant with me.

my father graduated a little while before i was born and got a job at applied materials as an engineer. the day that i was born, my father was in california for work, he came back to see me then had to return back to california the next day to work. for a month, my mother took care of her first newborn, me, on her own.

fast forward three years, and my mother became pregnant with my little brother. by this time, my father was making enough money to own a small house. with this and the idea of sending both of their children to decent schools in mind, my parents moved to pflugerville, texas and built a small house there.

twenty years later, i am at a university studying to be a physician's assistant and my little brother is graduating high school this year as an honors student. my mother was a business owner for fifteen years and my father still works for applied materials as a lead engineer.

with the background and struggles of my parents in mind, both my brother and i strive to make sure that our parents will always hold immense pride within us and never have any regrets about the decisions that they have made for our lives. this book represents just a small fraction of the values that my parents have instilled within me and values that i will keep in my heart for as long as i live.

nirali amin

i am filled with satisfaction

as many roads are crystal clear,

i look up, it's an illusion

\-   *there are no choices*

i

demon

the world is
not a fair
place.
everyone is
out to get me.
no one wants
to see me
succeed. i
work and
work only to
be handed
nothing in
return. i
always get the
short end of
the stick.

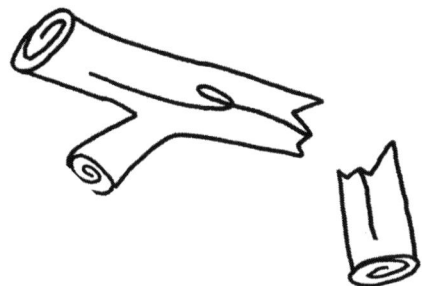

dismantled

i cannot
control the
things that
happen to me.
there is more
darkness than
there is light
within the
world. i live in
a world where
my opinion
matters to no
one. i exist
only to please
everyone but
myself.

i have no one
because no
one likes me.
everyone uses
me to their
advantage
only to end up
leaving me
when things
become
rough. what
did i do to
deserve this
life? i live
only to end up
dead one day.

these are
things that we
tell ourselves
in order to
make us feel
as if life is not
in our own
hands. as if all
unfortunate
things happen
just because.
as if the world
is out to get
us. as if life
was only
granted to us
so that we can
repay the debt
that we have
collected in
our past lives.

dismantled

sometimes,
life seems
unbearable
without telling
ourselves
these things.
other times,
life seems
unbearable
because we
tell ourselves
these things so
often that we
begin to
believe them.

dismantled

we live in a
world with an
enormous
demon. a
demon that
makes us cry
ourselves to
sleep every
night. a
demon that
makes us feel
miniscule to
those around
us.

a demon that
makes life a
living hell.
this demon
lives within
each and
every one of
us.
your demon
is you.

nirali amin

·

an empty vase sits alone,

never recognized, never touched.

soon, broken and disowned

\-   *loneliness kills*

ii

faith

in the most
abstract of
terms, religion
can be defined
as a belief
system put
into place by
mankind in
order to create
a balanced
and uniform
practice of
faith.
thousands of
different
religions are
practiced by
human beings
throughout the
world. which
religion is the
correct
religion?

dismantled

many people would
agree that there is no
one correct religion.
every religion has
one concept that is
the same. this
concept is that there
is a higher,
supernatural, power.

so, i ask again,
which religion is
correct? religion
is something that
was created by
mankind to give
humanity hope
and a way to
practice their
faith. do not
negate that a
higher power
exists. however,
this higher power
did not come into
existence as
stated within the
bible,
mahabharata,
quran or any
other holy book.
god came to
existence in a
way that no soul
on this earth
would be able to
comprehend.

36

nirali amin

i was born and
raised as hindu
while many of
my close friends
were brought up
as muslim. there
are many rules,
restrictions and
fasting rituals
related to both the
islamic and hindu
religions. why
would one
commit to fasting
when it could
potentially harm
one's health?
what kind of god
would want us to
kill ourselves for
him or her? if we
are the children
of god, we should
do all things that
are beneficial to
us.

dismantled

with this being
said, i am not
against fasting. i
have committed
to fasting and will
continue to do so.
however, if you
are physically
incapable of
fasting, god is not
telling you to kill
yourself for him
or her.

an indian spiritual
leader and
philanthropist,
sathya sai baba,
stated, "god is the
mother and father of
the world. our
parents are the
mother and father of
this body. god is
one; there are not
many gods, one for
each tribe among
men."

there are not many
gods. god is one. no
religion should be
bashed for their
beliefs. each religion
is a vessel through
which humankind
can express their
faith for this higher
power, for god.
every religion is
beautiful and
mankind is beautiful
for creating the
concept of religion.
through religion, we
have a way of
expressing our
vulnerability and our
faith to god.

nirali amin

in the woods lies a building,

inside, a wooden engraving

"who am i?" it was me.

-   a past life

iii

harmony

there is no
greater
feeling
than the
feeling of
immense
pride and
love for
one's
country.
each and
every
country on
earth is a
beautiful
work of
art.

.

dismantled

mankind
has filled
this
ravishing
planet with
foul
stereotypes
regarding
each and
every
country.
why?

human beings
have been
committing
themselves to
combat against
other countries
for many
centuries.
homo sapiens,
modern human
beings, are the
most dominant
species on this
planet, yet, we
live through the
hatred of each
other.

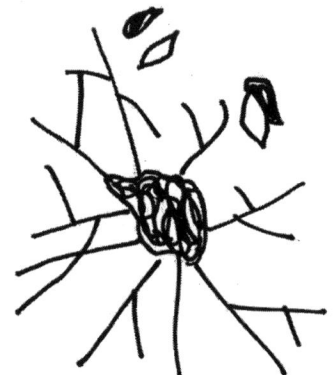

we live in a
world that
dehumanizes
those who
receive a pay
grade lower than
the average
individual. we
live in a world
where the color
of one's skin
becomes their
personal profile.
we live in a
world where we
are judged for
expressing
ourselves
through our
unique way of
thinking. should
we sit in silence
and simply
assimilate to this
shattered
mindset of
society?

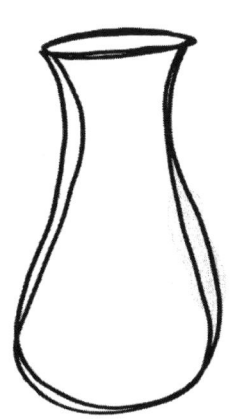

imagine a life
within which
war did not
exist. imagine a
life where skin
color did not
make a
difference in
the character of
a person.
imagine a life
where each
country lived in
harmony.
imagine a life
with a society
that only knows
happiness,
appreciation,
respect and
pride. why do
we not live a
life like this?

dismantle the
human bodies
of various
individuals
across different
ethnicities and
countries. what
will you find?
an anatomical
structure that
bears great
resemblance to
one another.

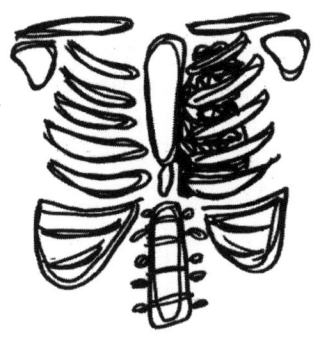

each human
being has been
created in the
same way. each
human being
has a heart,
about the size
of a fist, that
pumps blood
throughout the
body. each
human being
was carried in
their mother's
uterus before
being
introduced to
the delicacy
and complexity
of this world.
we are one.

nirali amin

.

lust is a forbidden fruit,

knowing this, you thirst even more

you use her, like a whore

- *temptation*

iv

enlightenment

education is a
beautiful gift.
the more you
know and learn,
the less there is
in the world
that you do not
know.

i am a child of
immigrant
parents. my
parents got
married in india
and moved to
the states in
order to provide
a future full of
opportunities,
hope and
education for
their unborn
children. they
sacrificed
everything in
order to ensure
a brighter
future. i,
personally, am
overjoyed and
beyond grateful
to be studying
at a university
and to be on a
path to make
something
greater out of
myself.

there are people
in today's
world who
would be
willing to give
up anything and
everything for a
chance to
receive an
education.
meanwhile, in
the states, we
take education
for granted. we
see education
as something
that we pursue
for a paycheck.
education is not
a person's
gateway to a
paycheck, but a
gateway to your
brain's
capabilities.

growing and
discovering
one's own
beliefs and
values is
something that
is done through
gaining an
education. the
more you learn,
the more
refined your
beliefs will
become. one
will be able to
understand
some of the
most complex
questions on
this earth.

questions like,
why does the
human body
function the
way that it
does? why does
an object return
to the ground
after it is
thrown
upwards into
the air? why is
a majority of
the earth made
up of water?
why do people
lie? why do we
have dreams?
why do people
act the way that
they do? why is
society the way
that it is?

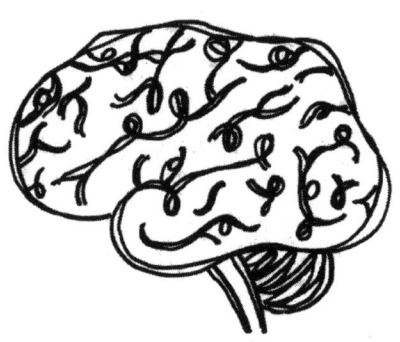

the brain is an
untapped organ.
the brain holds
all of the
knowledge we
have gained
throughout the
years. the brain
is the key to an
education which
is, in return, the
key to
understanding
ourselves.

dismantled

i encourage everyone to go out and get
an education in order to see the great
potential that you hold. get an
education, find the reason for which
god has put you onto this planet, then
begin to pursue that reason and make
your life meaningful.

nirali amin

a grotesque, frightful flame grows,

fuming with smoke, the air darkens

without warning, it snows

\-   *temper*

v

superiority

there is a
population of
approximately
seven billion
human beings
on this plant.
picture all
seven billion
people
believing that
they are
superior to the
individuals
that they are
surrounded by.
that was not
very hard to
picture, was it?

this scenario is
not very difficult
to imagine
because,
essentially, we
live in a society
within which
most mortal
beings are
strikingly
egocentric. we
prance around
this earth
judging people
by their body
weight, skin
color, facial
features,
paycheck and so
much more. if an
individual has a
need to judge
people based on
these things for
personal
satisfaction, then
they have yet to
discover the
journey to
reaching self-
actualization.

people who
carry
themselves
believing that
they are more
powerful than
others are
people who do
not understand
that every
human being
is powerful.
power does
not come from
the position
you hold
within your
career, the title
held behind
your name or
from raising
your voice.
power comes
from within

power comes to a human being
when one finds the ability to gain
control of their own life. being
able to live your life the way that
you please and being able to
surround yourself with only the
type of people that you choose is,
in my opinion, true power. power
is not about making the
individuals around you feel as if
they are inferior to you, or about
feeling superior to others.

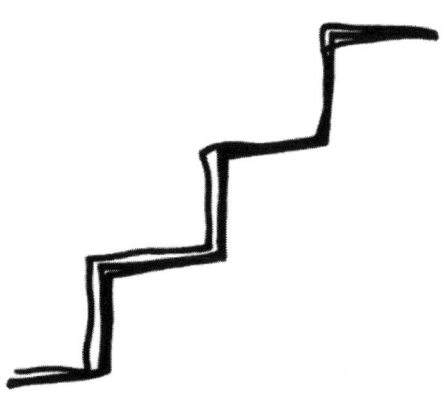

god filled the
world with so
many living
souls, so that all
of us could live
in unity to make
this world
everything that it
should be. living
a life within
which one's goal
is to feel
superior, is a life
wasted. no
human being is
neither superior
nor inferior to
another.

the mentality of
superiority is
what could
possibly result in
the destruction of
the world that
god had intended.
being able to
treat others with
the utmost
respect, and
being able to
truly understand
equality will
guide one onto an
enlightening path
which will only
make one's life
more meaningful.

nirali amin

.

a brisk chill rushes through me,

i am capable, i am free

i am not under lock and key

- *freedom*

vi

angel

the world is a fair
place if i make it
one. i want what
is best for myself.
i want to see
myself succeed. i
will work so that
i can fulfill my
passion. a
positive attitude
can ensure a
positive outcome.

i am able to
take my life
into my own
hands. i will
build my
own destiny.
i have the
power to fill
the world
with light.
my opinions
are what
make me. i
exist to live
a marvelous
life.

dismantled

.

i am loved.
everyone that i
choose to
surround myself
with makes me
powerful. i
deserve this life. i
live for
happiness.

these are the
things that we
should be
telling
ourselves
every day.
along with
our demon,
another being
resides within
each and
every one of
us. a force
that is often
overlooked by
us. this vital
force is an
angel.

according to
human nature,
we tend to
believe in the
negative
versus the
positive. we
let the demon
overpower the
angel within
us, making
this one of the
biggest
weaknesses of
each living
soul.

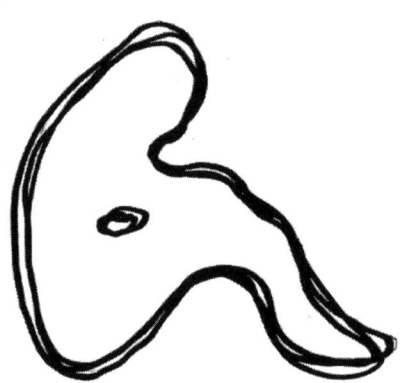

let the angel
conquer the
demon and
see what a
difference this
can make in
your life.
what goes
around comes
around. what
one can give
out into the
world is what
he or she shall
receive in
return.

in conclusion,
give good and
take
possession of
the good
given in
return.

nirali amin

thank you...